OLSAT® Practice Test (Kindergarten and Grade 1)

Includes Tips for preparing for the OLSAT® Test

Authored, written by: Bright Minds Publishing

Bright Minds Publishing

Contents

Introduction to OLSAT®

Introduction

The OLSAT® is widely used throughout the United States as a test for entry into the Gifted and Talented program. Pearson Assessments describe their test for Kindergarten and Grade 1 as follows:

Area	Type	Skill Tested
Verbal	Verbal Comprehension	Following Direction
	Verbal Reasoning	Aural Reasoning
		Arithmetic Reasoning
Non Verbal	Pictorial Reasoning	Picture Classification
		Picture Analogies
		Picture Series
	Figural Reasoning	Figural Classification
		Figural Analogies
		Pattern Matrix
		Figure Series

Structure of OLSAT® Test.

The OLSAT® test consists of the following 4 sections. Each test has a certain time allocated to finish the questions.

Section Name	Number of Questions	Minutes (Approximate)
Section1: Verbal Comprehension	12	15
Section 2: Verbal Reasoning	12	15
Section 3: Pictorial Reasoning	16	15
Section 4: Figural Reasoning	20	15
Total	60	~1 hour

Kindergarten entry students are administered Section 1, 2 and 3 only.

1st Grade entry students are administered all sections.

Tips for parents on how to prepare your child for OLSAT® Test

1. Start planning early so that you can take a practice test, and get your child aware about the format of the test. Administer this test and watch for areas where your child needs improvement.

2. Take examples and explain to your child what concept is tested in each section. What children need most are examples and practice.

3. Administer this test in 2 or 3 sessions. Children have varying attention spans and they will need some time to adapt to the format of the test and pay attention to each section. If you child is a bit distracted then take a break and come back to the test when your child is fresh and able to concentrate.

4. Teach your child how to mark the right answer on the answer sheet. Make them practice marking the right answer.

5. Review the questions and the answers marked by your child. Explain to them why a question is answered incorrectly. Revisit all the questions they marked wrong in a few days to see if they have grasped the concept.

Instructions on administering OLSAT® Test

1. Time each section. It is important for you to progress through the section in the time provided. It is important to make progress but don't hurry or stress your child.

2. Read each question to your child. Read the question exactly the way it reads.

3. Do not provide your child with the meaning of the question or hints about how to solve the question during the initial testing. You will have the opportunity to do so when reviewing their answers.

4. Repeat the question in case your child did not hear the question right.

5. Once your child has determined the right answer, ensure they mark the bubble in the right way.

6. After the test has been administered, check the answers and explain to your child what the questions meant and why the answers were incorrect (in case they are incorrect). Explain to your child what the correct answer is and why it is the correct answer.

7. When new concepts are introduced to children, give them multiple examples of the concept. Refresh the concepts after a few days, every few days to help them remember.

Practice Test 1

Section 1: Verbal Comprehension

Section 1: Verbal Comprehension

Instructions:

Here is a sample question in this section:

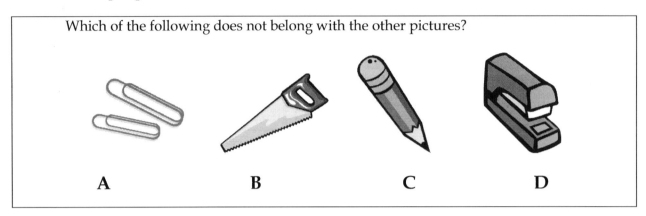

Which of the following does not belong with the other pictures?

| A | B | C | D |

Read the question. See the four images. Think about what has been asked in the questions. On the blank answer sheet at the end of this book, pencil in the correct bubble to answer the question.

The correct answer here is option B because all other items are used either in a home or office. The saw does not belong with the other three items.

All the questions in this section can be solved in the same manner.

1. Which of the following does not belong with the other pictures?

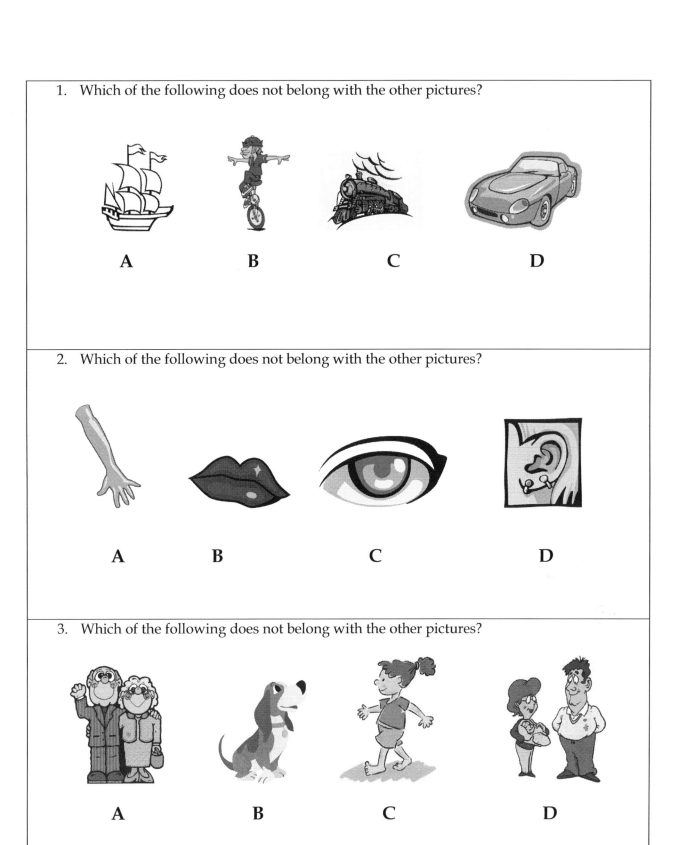

A

B

C

D

2. Which of the following does not belong with the other pictures?

A

B

C

D

3. Which of the following does not belong with the other pictures?

A

B

C

D

4. Which of the following does not belong with the other pictures?

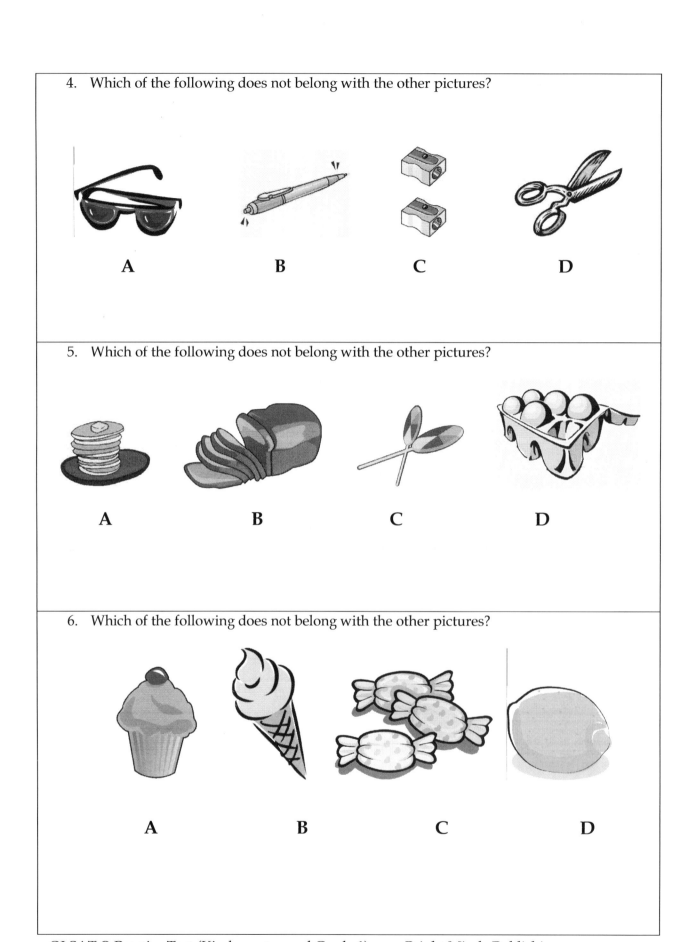

A B C D

5. Which of the following does not belong with the other pictures?

A B C D

6. Which of the following does not belong with the other pictures?

A B C D

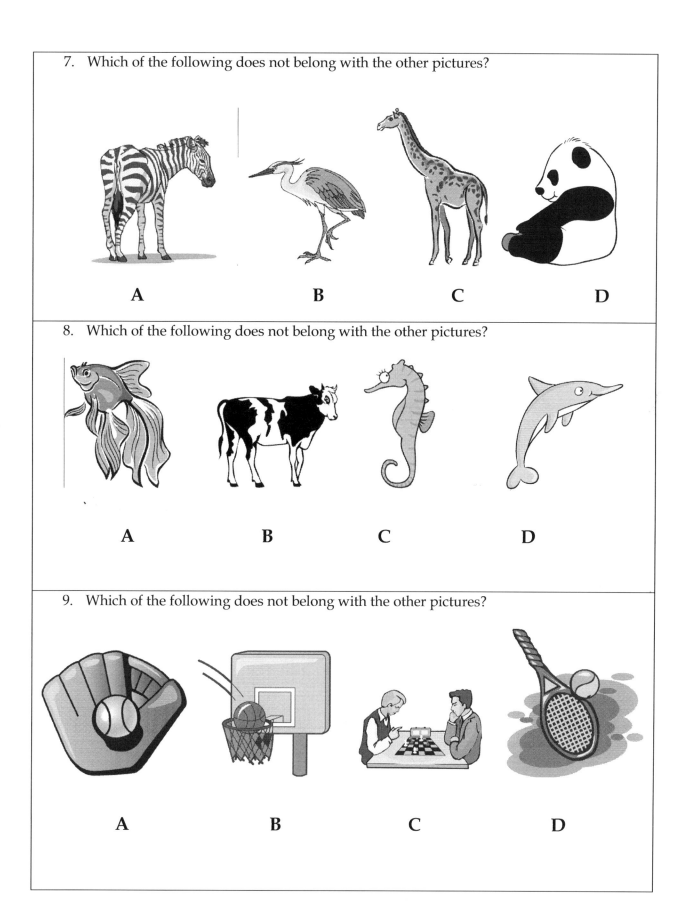

7. Which of the following does not belong with the other pictures?

A   B   C   D

8. Which of the following does not belong with the other pictures?

A   B   C   D

9. Which of the following does not belong with the other pictures?

A   B   C   D

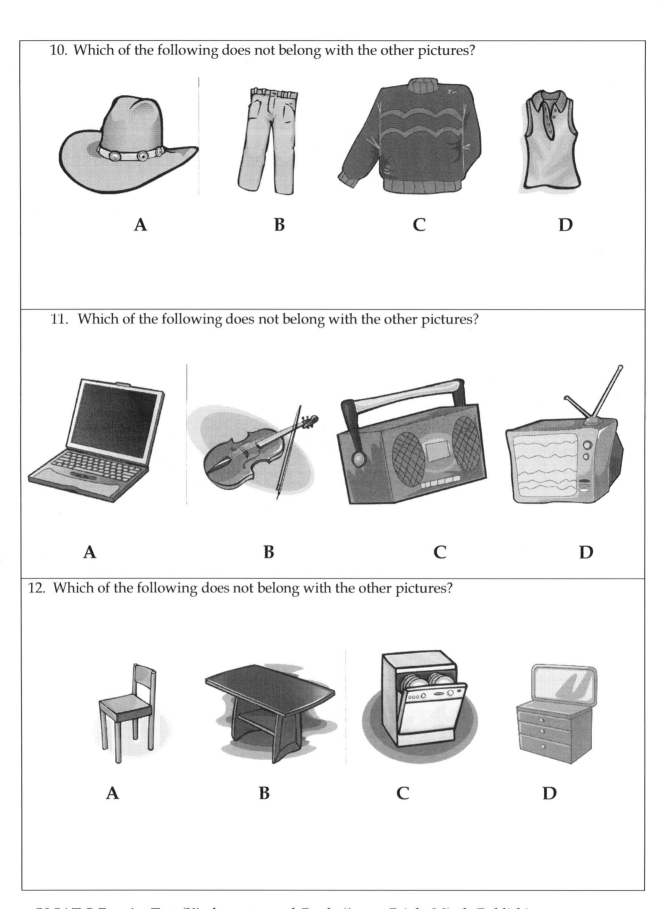

10. Which of the following does not belong with the other pictures?

A   B   C   D

11. Which of the following does not belong with the other pictures?

A   B   C   D

12. Which of the following does not belong with the other pictures?

A   B   C   D

Section 2: Verbal Reasoning

Section 2: Verbal Reasoning

Instructions:

Here is a sample question in this section:

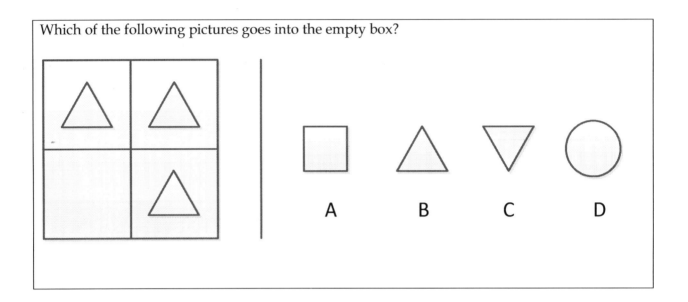

Read the question. See the four images. See the objects inside the square box. Now see the answer options A through D. Decide which answer is the option. On the blank answer sheet at the end of this book, pencil in the bubble to answer the question.

The correct answer here is option B because all the images inside the square box on the left are triangles with the base below and tip directed vertically up.

All the questions in this section can be solved in the same manner.

1. Which of the following pictures goes into the empty box?

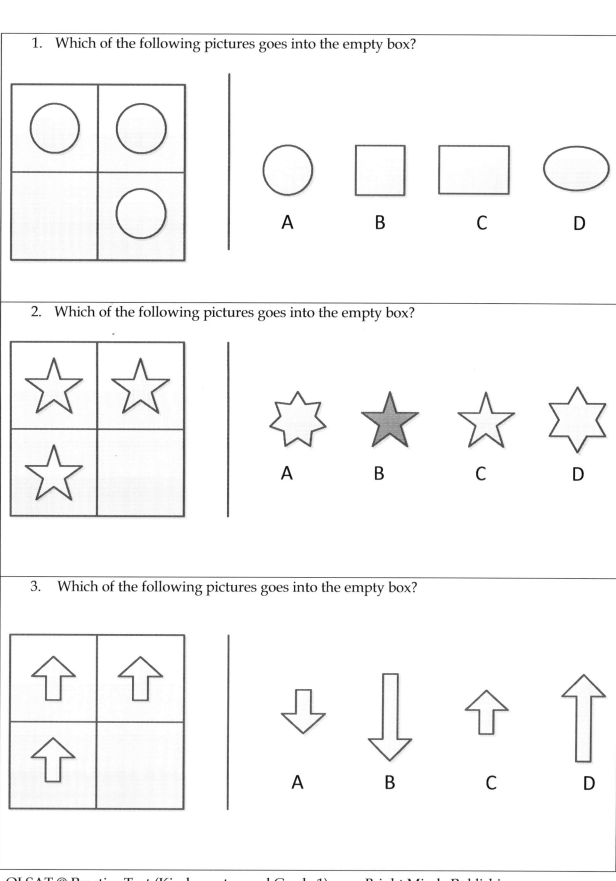

2. Which of the following pictures goes into the empty box?

3. Which of the following pictures goes into the empty box?

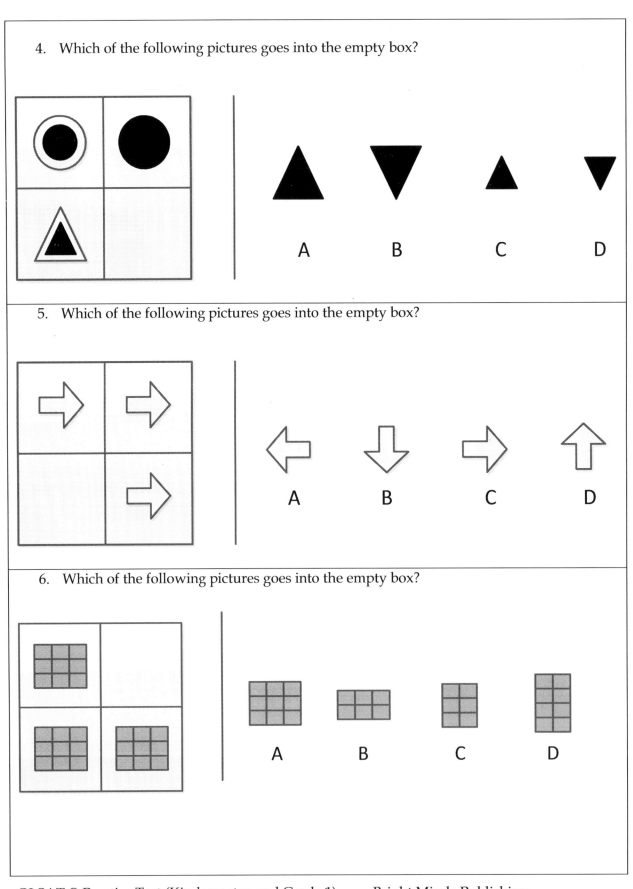

4. Which of the following pictures goes into the empty box?

A   B   C   D

5. Which of the following pictures goes into the empty box?

A   B   C   D

6. Which of the following pictures goes into the empty box?

A   B   C   D

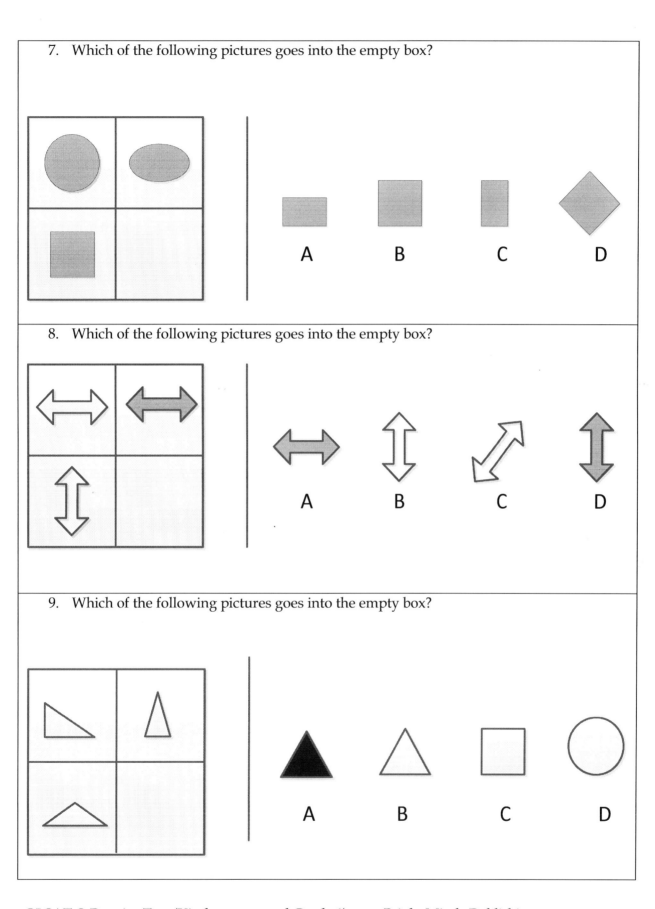

7. Which of the following pictures goes into the empty box?

A B C D

8. Which of the following pictures goes into the empty box?

A B C D

9. Which of the following pictures goes into the empty box?

A B C D

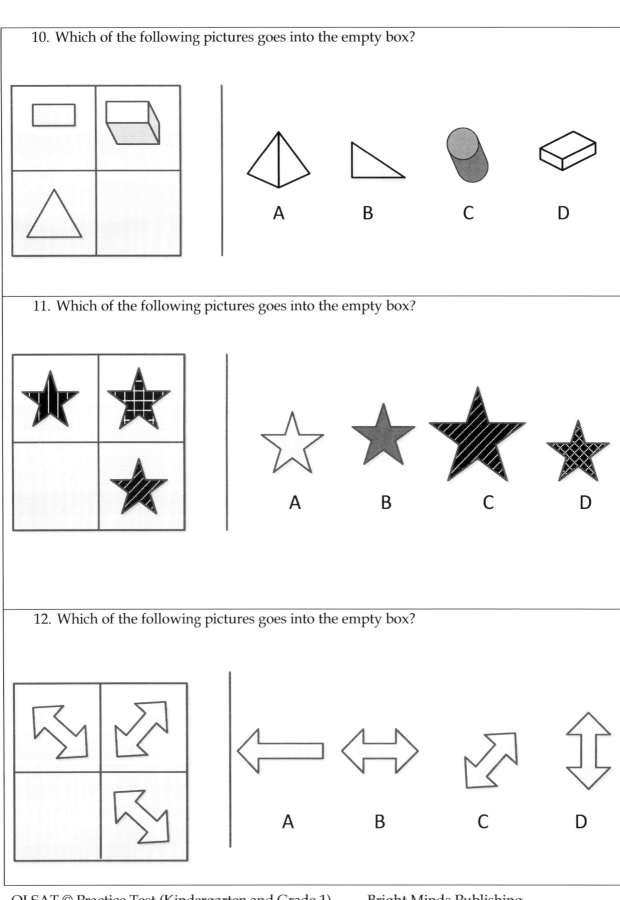

10. Which of the following pictures goes into the empty box?

A   B   C   D

11. Which of the following pictures goes into the empty box?

A   B   C   D

12. Which of the following pictures goes into the empty box?

A   B   C   D

Section 3: Pictorial Reasoning

Section 3: Pictorial Reasoning

Here is a sample question in this section:

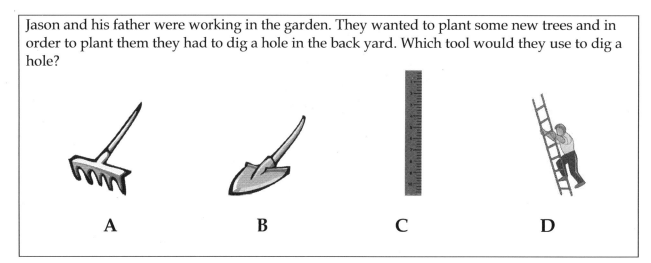

Jason and his father were working in the garden. They wanted to plant some new trees and in order to plant them they had to dig a hole in the back yard. Which tool would they use to dig a hole?

A   B   C   D

Read the question. See the four images. Try and figure out which of the following objects can be used to answer the question. On the blank answer sheet at the end of this book, pencil in the bubble to answer the question.

The correct answer here is option B because a shovel is used to dig a hole in the ground.

All the questions in this section can be solved in the same manner.

1 Corey went to the airport to take a flight to visit his grandmother with her 3 brothers and parents. When he got to the airport he saw a lot of things that took off and landed. He even boarded one to go to his grandmother. Which is it?

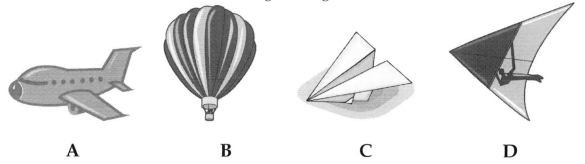

A   **B**   **C**   **D**

2. Nancy celebrated her birthday party with her family and friends. She cut this thing during her party. Each of her friends got a slice of this sweet thing. Which was it?

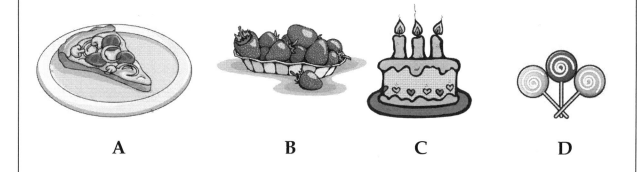

A   **B**   **C**   **D**

3. Zach went to get some groceries with his father. They got some fruits from the store. They got strawberries, pear and apples. They got fewer pears than strawberries and they got more apples than strawberries. Which fruit is the most in number?

A   **B**   **C**   **D**

4. Misty likes to play with her toys in her room. One of her favorite toys is a soft toy that is an animal. Which is it?

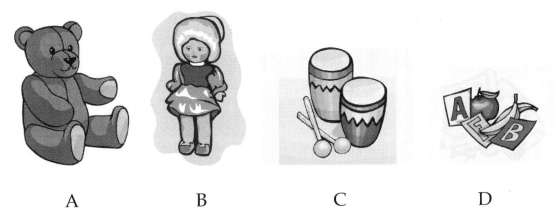

A   B   C   D

5. Every evening the kids love to play on the swing, jungle gym and other play equipment in the park. Which of the following is **not** something they would find in the park that is safe for children?

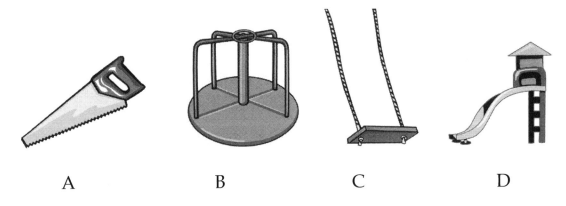

A   B   C   D

6. In order to get to school, Ann has to take a school bus that picks her up outside her house. The bus also picks up several other children in the neighborhood. Which of the following shows how she will get to school?

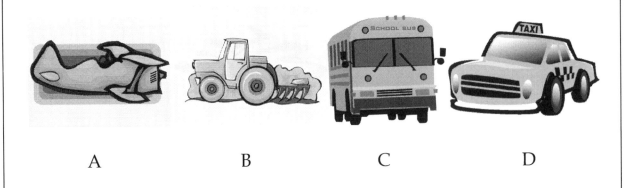

A   B   C   D

7. Alaethia visited the park in the evening. She saw 4 dragon flies in one of the flower patches. 2 dragon flies flew away and then in few minutes 1 dragon fly flew back into the flower patch. Alaethia had to leave the park since it got dark. How many dragon flies were in the flower patch when Alaethia left the park?

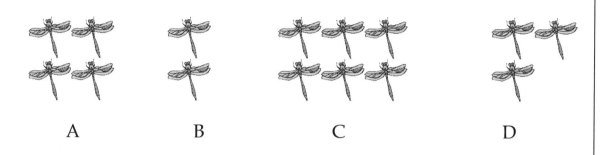

    A   B   C   D

8. After playing all afternoon in the sun, the kids were very thirsty and asked for something that they can drink to quench their thirst. What did they ask for?

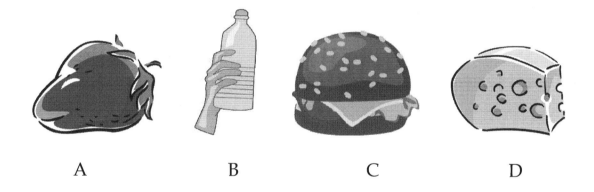

    A   B   C   D

9. During her annual checkup with the doctor, Amanda was told by the doctor to drink a glass of milk with her regular breakfast before she headed off to middle school. Which of the following shows the amount of milk she will drink before heading off to school?

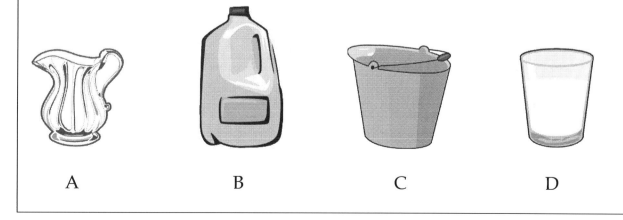

    A   B   C   D

10. See the 4 images below. These are gold coins stacked up in different ways. Which figure has the fewest number of coins?

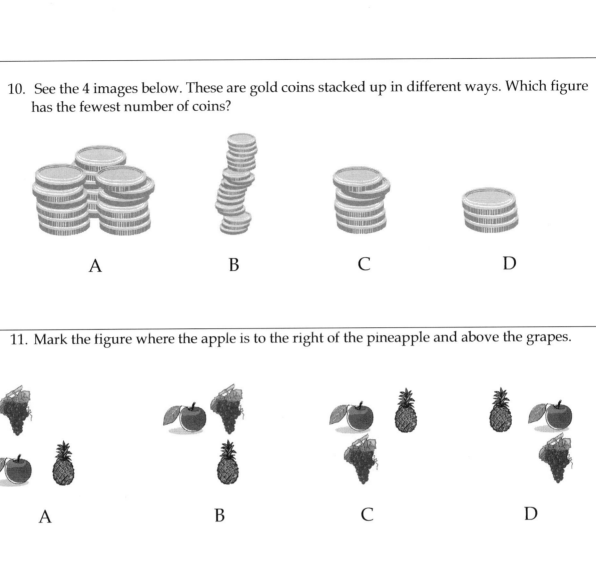

A   B   C   D

11. Mark the figure where the apple is to the right of the pineapple and above the grapes.

A   B   C   D

12. See the 4 images on the left side of the line. Which object is to the NORTH of the circle?

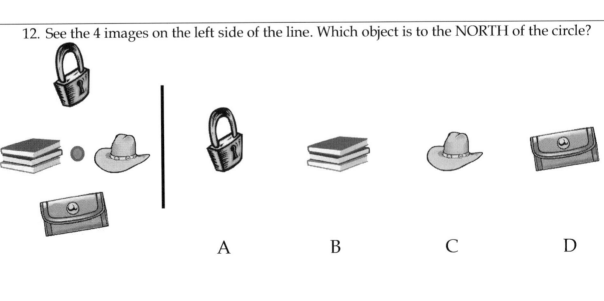

A   B   C   D

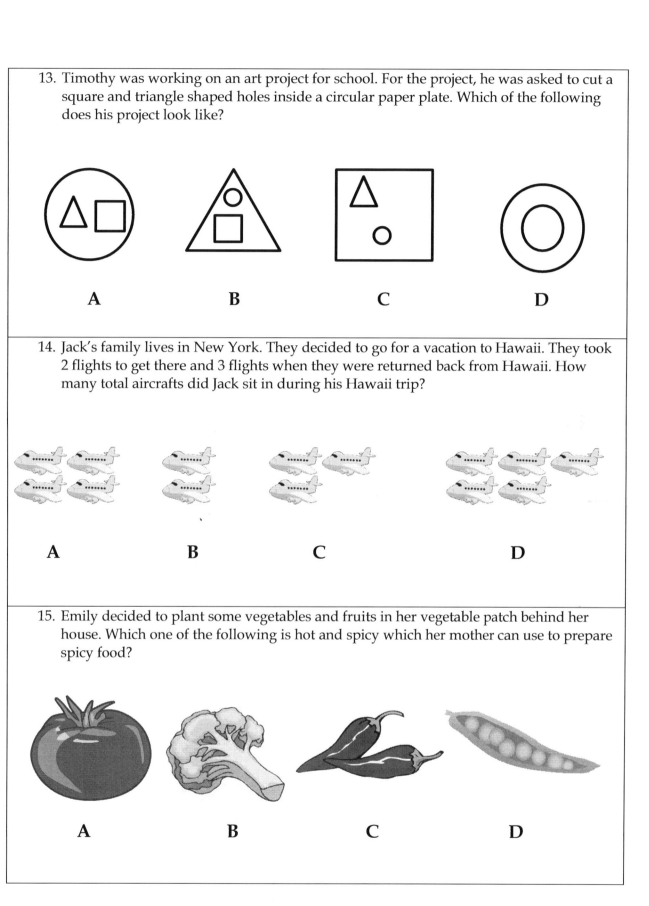

13. Timothy was working on an art project for school. For the project, he was asked to cut a square and triangle shaped holes inside a circular paper plate. Which of the following does his project look like?

A   B   C   D

14. Jack's family lives in New York. They decided to go for a vacation to Hawaii. They took 2 flights to get there and 3 flights when they were returned back from Hawaii. How many total aircrafts did Jack sit in during his Hawaii trip?

A   B   C   D

15. Emily decided to plant some vegetables and fruits in her vegetable patch behind her house. Which one of the following is hot and spicy which her mother can use to prepare spicy food?

A   B   C   D

16. Jessica Johnson has a younger brother Alex Johnson. Alex is taller than Jessica. Jessica's mother Alicia is taller than Alex. Which picture below would be the right picture for the family?

A   **B**   **C**   **D**

Section 4: Figural Reasoning

Section 4: Figural Reasoning

Instructions:

Read the question below and see the images. Count the number of apples with each option.

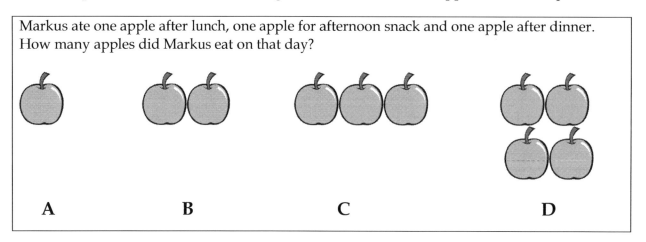

The correct answer here is Option C because the total count of apples that Markus ate on that day is 3 and option C has 3 apples.

All the questions in this section can be solved in the same manner.

1. Mary had 3 dolls that she got as presents for her birthday party from all her friends. She takes very good care of her dolls. Later that year when her grandmother was visiting her, she got her 1 more doll. How many dolls does she have now?

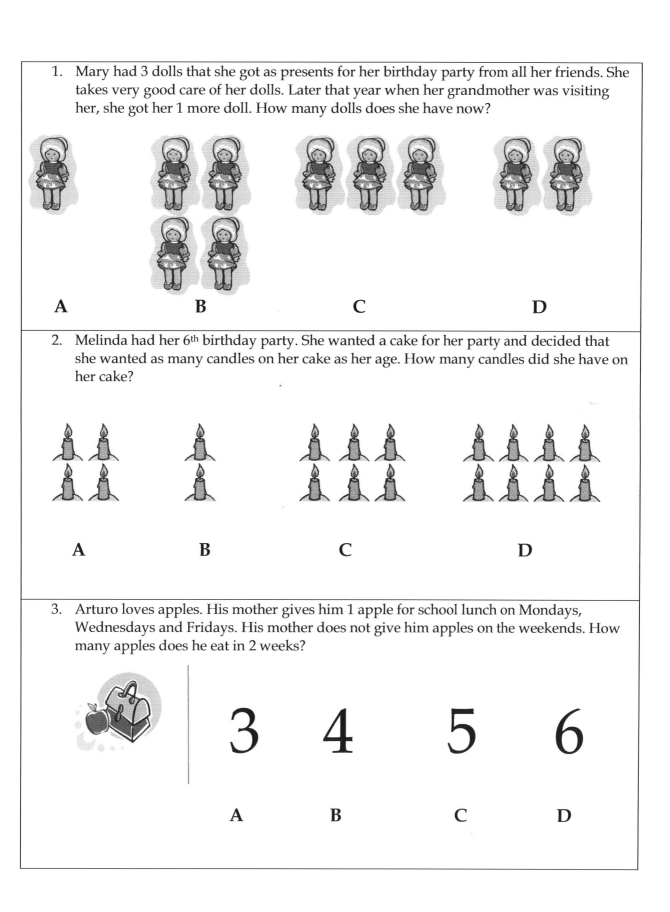

A   B   C   D

2. Melinda had her 6th birthday party. She wanted a cake for her party and decided that she wanted as many candles on her cake as her age. How many candles did she have on her cake?

A   B   C   D

3. Arturo loves apples. His mother gives him 1 apple for school lunch on Mondays, Wednesdays and Fridays. His mother does not give him apples on the weekends. How many apples does he eat in 2 weeks?

3   4   5   6

A   B   C   D

4. See the 4 objects below. There are some objects that are placed vertically, horizontally and other directions. Which object is positioned vertically?

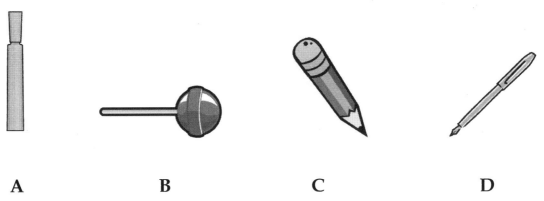

A   **B**   **C**   **D**

5. See the figures of donuts below. Annie decided to share the donuts with her friends but they did not want to eat the entire donut each. Her mother cut it into small pieces. Which donut is cut into the most number of pieces?

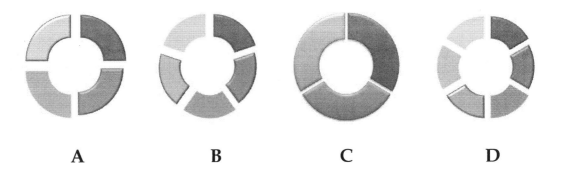

A   **B**   **C**   **D**

6. See the 4 figures below. There are some object placed inside the circle or triangle and some objects placed outside the circle or triangle. Mark the figure where the pencil is inside the circle.

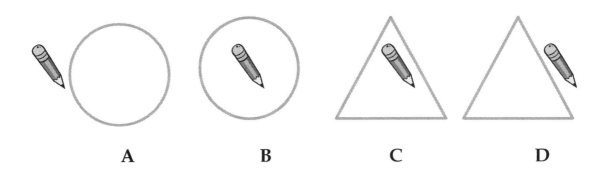

A   **B**   **C**   **D**

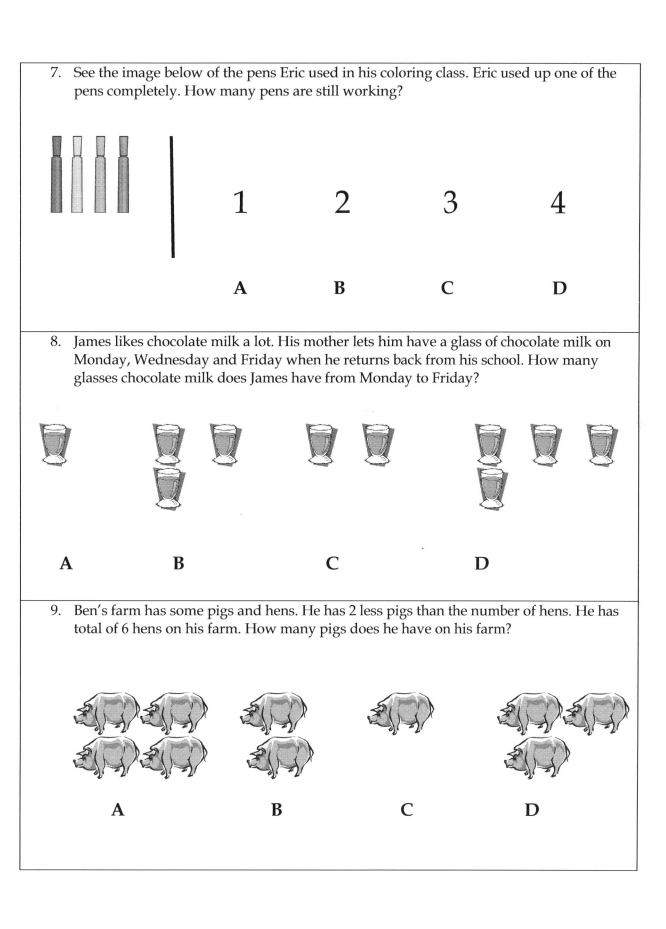

7. See the image below of the pens Eric used in his coloring class. Eric used up one of the pens completely. How many pens are still working?

1   2   3   4

A   B   C   D

8. James likes chocolate milk a lot. His mother lets him have a glass of chocolate milk on Monday, Wednesday and Friday when he returns back from his school. How many glasses chocolate milk does James have from Monday to Friday?

A   B   C   D

9. Ben's farm has some pigs and hens. He has 2 less pigs than the number of hens. He has total of 6 hens on his farm. How many pigs does he have on his farm?

A   B   C   D

10. Marion's mother is distributing cake to all his friends sitting at a round table. She told the kids that she would go round the table and distribute cake in clockwise direction. Which arrow below shows clock wise direction?

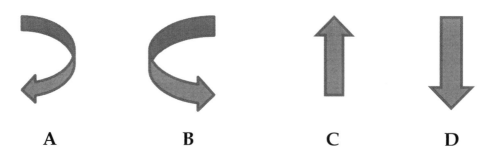

A   B   C   D

11. Michael wanted to figure out how strong he really is. So, his father asked him to check out the following objects and see which ones he can lift. Which object might likely be the heaviest for him to pick up?

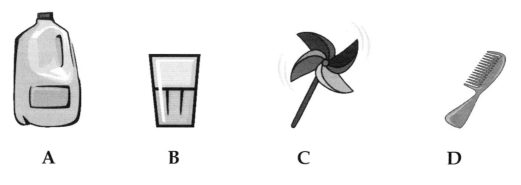

A   B   C   D

12. Angie was watching TV and the weather channel mentioned that the temperature was going to be very low that day and asked people to dress appropriately. What attire should Angie wear?

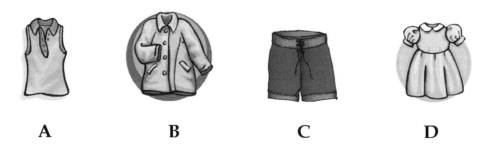

A   B   C   D

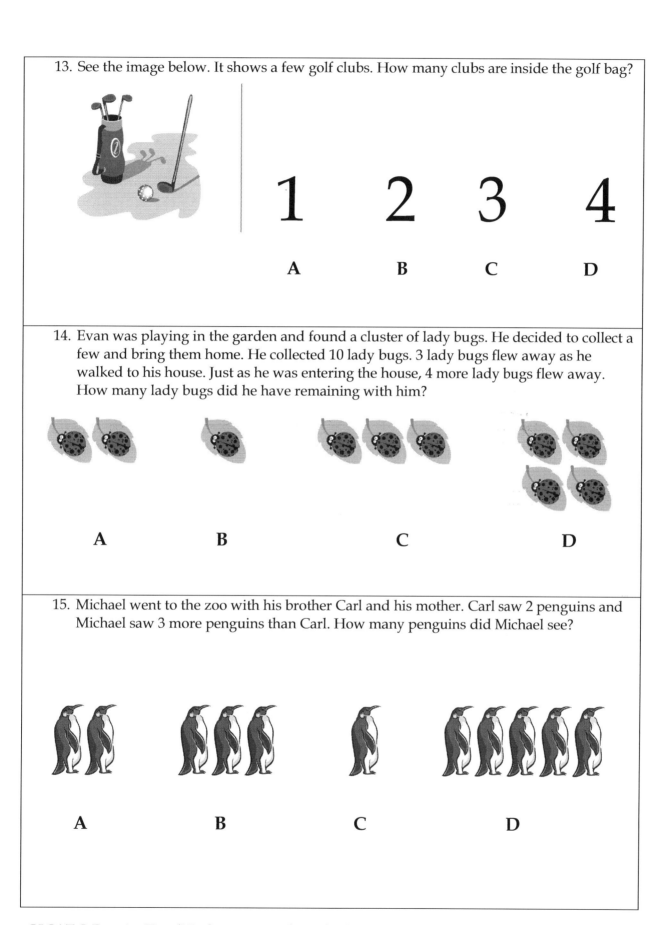

13. See the image below. It shows a few golf clubs. How many clubs are inside the golf bag?

1   2   3   4
A   B   C   D

14. Evan was playing in the garden and found a cluster of lady bugs. He decided to collect a few and bring them home. He collected 10 lady bugs. 3 lady bugs flew away as he walked to his house. Just as he was entering the house, 4 more lady bugs flew away. How many lady bugs did he have remaining with him?

A   B   C   D

15. Michael went to the zoo with his brother Carl and his mother. Carl saw 2 penguins and Michael saw 3 more penguins than Carl. How many penguins did Michael see?

A   B   C   D

16. See the 4 figures below. This picture shows 4 arrows. There are some that are thick, thin, long and short. Which arrow is the longest arrow?

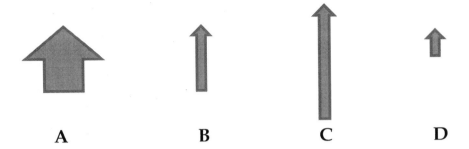

17. Amelia and her father went out fishing on a sunny afternoon at the local creek. They each caught 5 fish but they had to let 1 fish each back into the creek. How many fish did each of them bring back home?

18. Jonah's mother was making strawberry smoothies for Jonah and his sister Celia. Jonah wanted a full glass of smoothie and Celia wanted half a glass of smoothie. It turns out it takes 8 strawberries to make one full glass of smoothie. How many strawberries does Celia have in her half glass of smoothie?

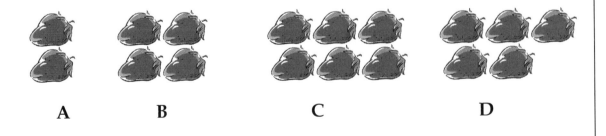

19. Marco went to a baseball game with his father. During the game his father caught one ball in the stands. After the game, his father purchased 2 more balls from the store. How many balls does Marco now have?

A	B	C	D

20. Mark is Marjorie's father. Mary is Marjorie's mother. Marjorie lived with her parents in their wonderful house. Mary and Mark just had another baby Mark Jr. How many people live in their house now?

2   3   4   5

A   B   C   D

Practice Test 2

Section 1: Verbal Comprehension

Section 1: Verbal Comprehension

Instructions:

Here is a sample question in this section:

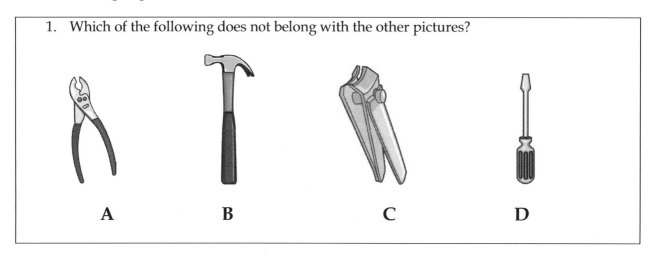

1. Which of the following does not belong with the other pictures?

      A   B   C   D

Read the question. Look at the four images. Think about what has been asked in the questions. On the blank answer sheet at the end of this book, pencil in the bubble to answer the question.

The correct answer here is option C because all other items are hardware tools used to mechanically fix things around the house where as the nail cutter is used to cut nails. The nail cutter doesn't belong with the other three items.

All the questions in this section can be solved in the same manner.

1. Which of the following does not belong with the other pictures?

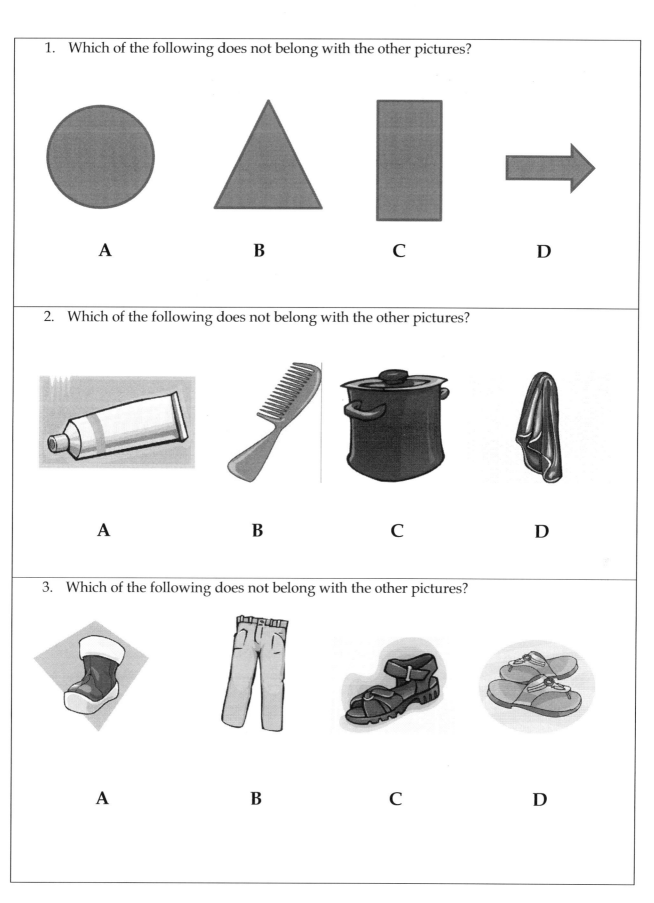

A   B   C   D

2. Which of the following does not belong with the other pictures?

A   B   C   D

3. Which of the following does not belong with the other pictures?

A   B   C   D

4. Which of the following does not belong with the other pictures?

A   B   C   D

5. Which of the following does not belong with the other pictures?

A   B   C   D

6. Which of the following does not belong with the other pictures?

A   B   C   D

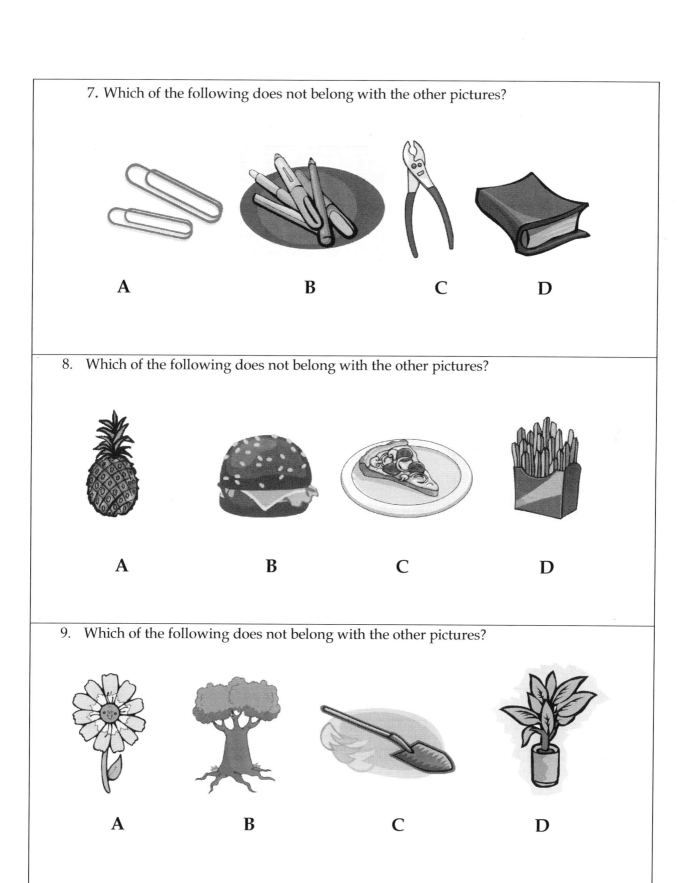

7. Which of the following does not belong with the other pictures?

A   B   C   D

8. Which of the following does not belong with the other pictures?

A   B   C   D

9. Which of the following does not belong with the other pictures?

A   B   C   D

10. Which of the following does not belong with the other pictures?

A **B** **C** **D**

11. Which of the following does not belong with the other pictures?

A B C D

12. Which of the following does not belong with the other pictures?

A B C D

Section 2: Verbal Reasoning

Section 2: Verbal Reasoning

Instructions:

Here is a sample question in this section:

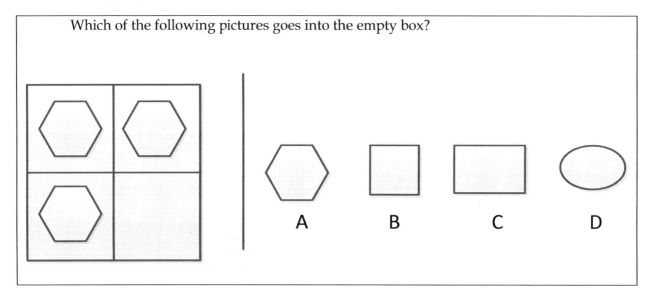

Which of the following pictures goes into the empty box?

A   B   C   D

See the 3 images on the left side of the line. Then see the 4 images on the right side of the line. See if there is a pattern for the images on the left side and figure out which images would complete the pattern on the left side.

The correct answer here is Option A because the objects on the left side have 6 sides and the object A has 6 sides.

All the questions in this section can be solved in the same manner.

1. Which of the following pictures goes into the empty box?

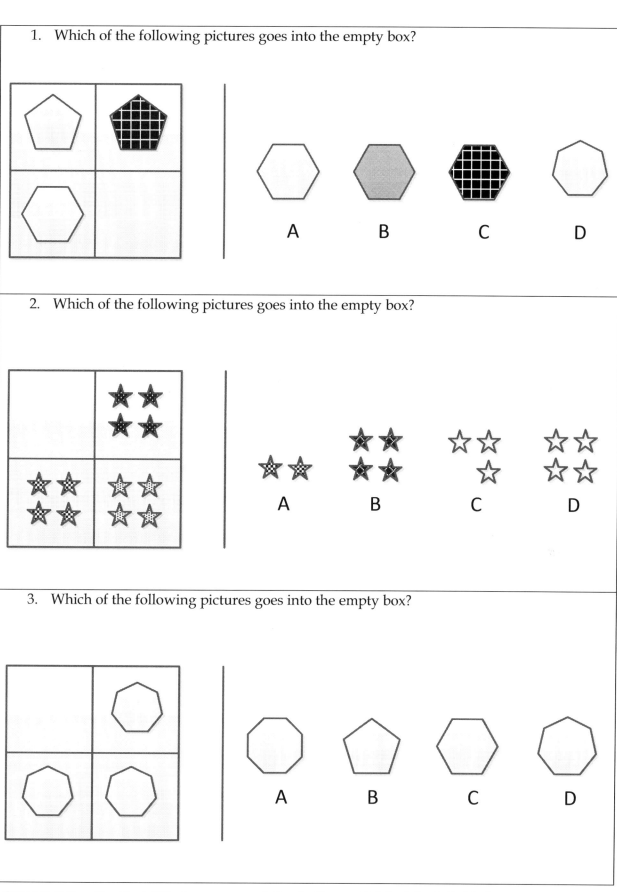

2. Which of the following pictures goes into the empty box?

3. Which of the following pictures goes into the empty box?

4. Which of the following pictures goes into the empty box?

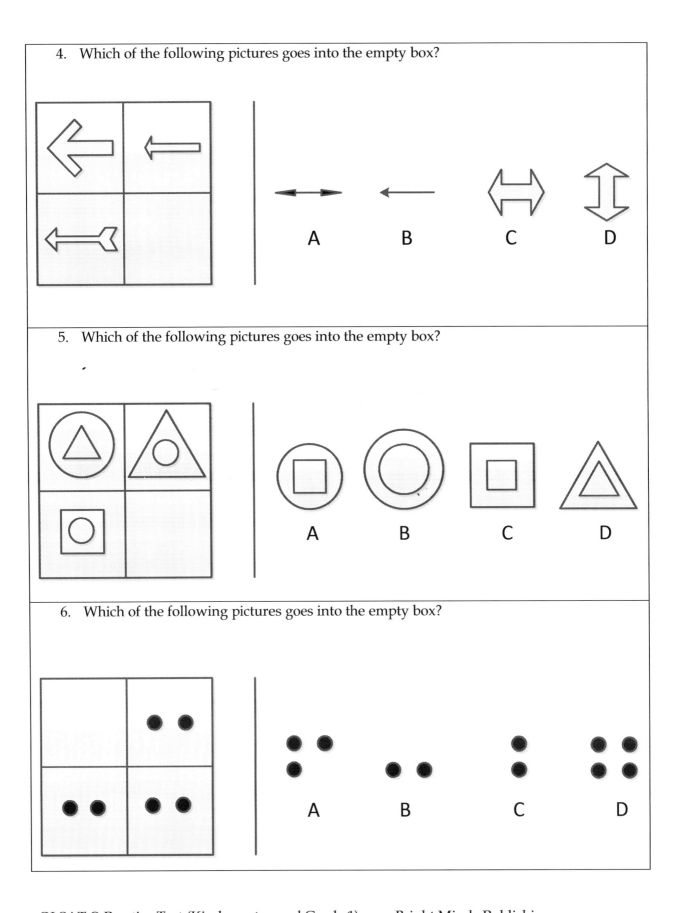

5. Which of the following pictures goes into the empty box?

6. Which of the following pictures goes into the empty box?

7. Which of the following pictures goes into the empty box?

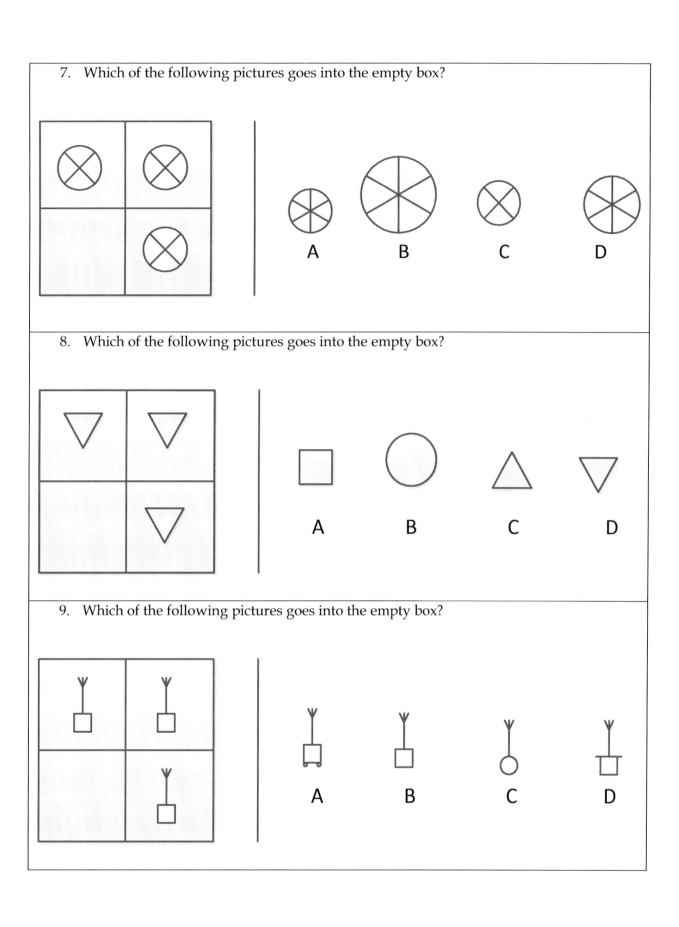

8. Which of the following pictures goes into the empty box?

9. Which of the following pictures goes into the empty box?

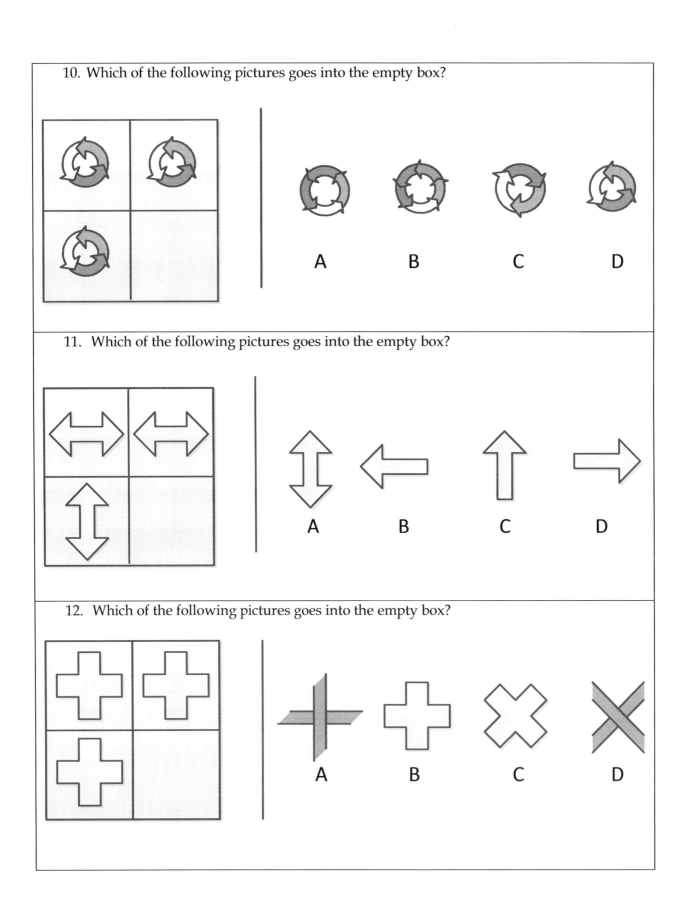

10. Which of the following pictures goes into the empty box?

A   B   C   D

11. Which of the following pictures goes into the empty box?

A   B   C   D

12. Which of the following pictures goes into the empty box?

A   B   C   D

Section 3: Pictorial Reasoning

Section 3: Pictorial Reasoning

Instructions:

Here is a sample question in this section:

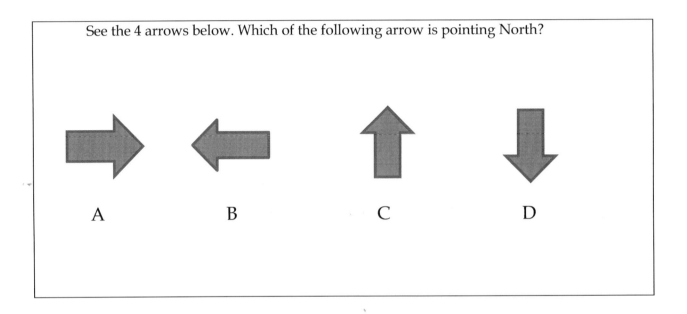

Read the question. See the 4 images. Then try to find out which images can be used to answer the question asked.

The correct answer here is option C because that is the only arrow pointing up.

All the questions in this section can be solved in the same manner.

1. Victoria got into trouble and was given a timeout and asked to spend the day in her room. She was not allowed to play with her video games or dolls or watch TV. Which is the one object she can use in her room during her timeout?

A   B   C   D

2. Mary's younger brother is 5 years old. Her older brother is 9 years old. How old can Mary be?

A   B   C   D

3. Rose decided to distribute 1 dum-dum to each of her three friends. She would take one and save one for her younger brother. How many dum-dums would she have to buy?

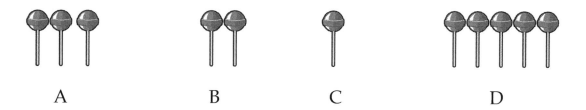

A   B   C   D

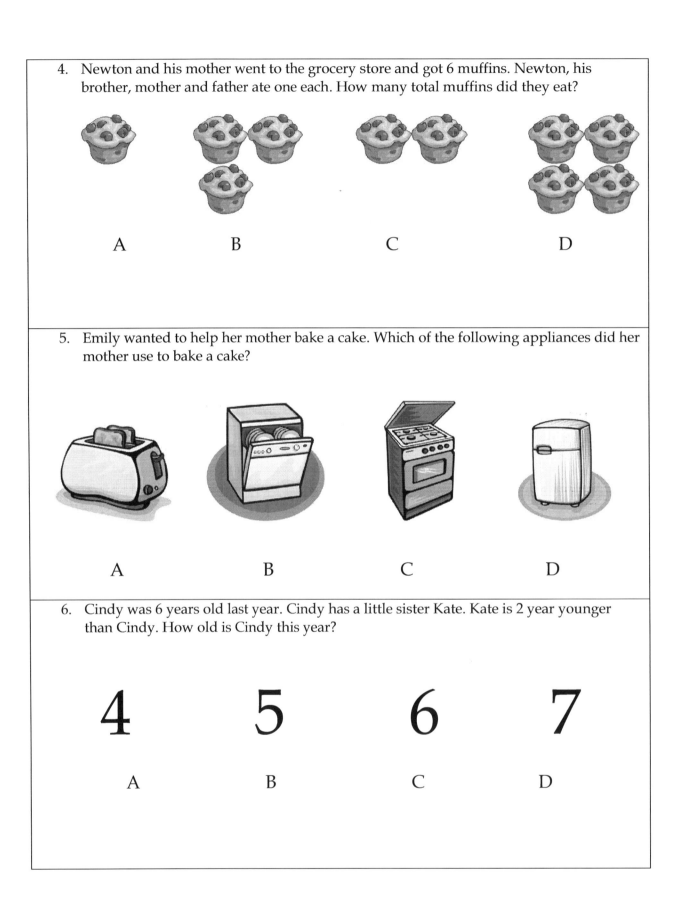

4. Newton and his mother went to the grocery store and got 6 muffins. Newton, his brother, mother and father ate one each. How many total muffins did they eat?

A   B   C   D

5. Emily wanted to help her mother bake a cake. Which of the following appliances did her mother use to bake a cake?

A   B   C   D

6. Cindy was 6 years old last year. Cindy has a little sister Kate. Kate is 2 year younger than Cindy. How old is Cindy this year?

4   5   6   7

A   B   C   D

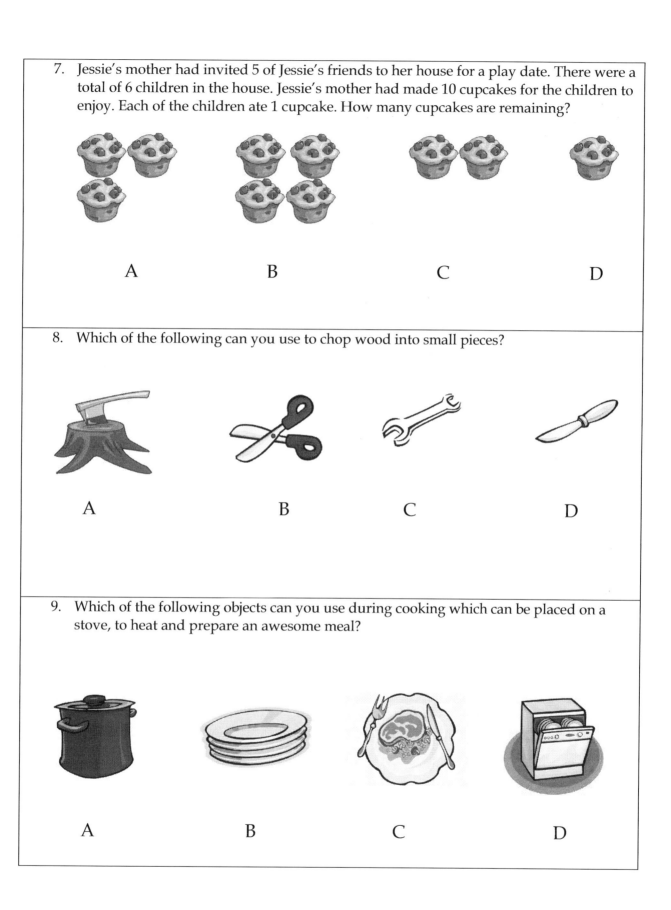

7. Jessie's mother had invited 5 of Jessie's friends to her house for a play date. There were a total of 6 children in the house. Jessie's mother had made 10 cupcakes for the children to enjoy. Each of the children ate 1 cupcake. How many cupcakes are remaining?

A   B   C   D

8. Which of the following can you use to chop wood into small pieces?

A   B   C   D

9. Which of the following objects can you use during cooking which can be placed on a stove, to heat and prepare an awesome meal?

A   B   C   D

10. Which of the following objects can a diver use to protect the eyes from water going into their eyes while diving?

A   B   C   D

11. Which of the following is a type of nut that you can crack open and eat as a snack?

A   B   C   D

12. Which of the following things can you put into a cup of coffee in order to make it sweet?

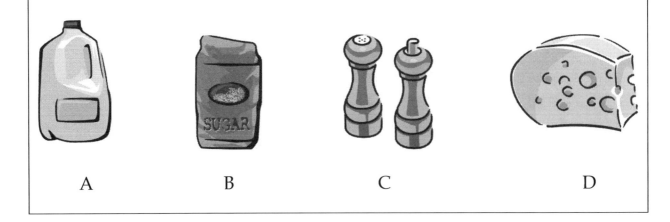

A   B   C   D

13. Which of the following items is a delicious fruit that you need to peel before you eat it?

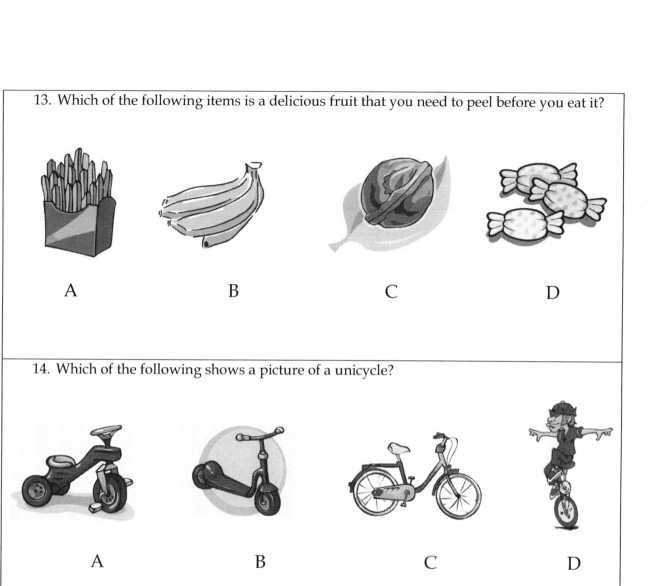

14. Which of the following shows a picture of a unicycle?

15. See the image of the box and the items placed near the box. There are some objects are on the box and some are placed on the side of the box. Which item is placed on the front and top side of the box?

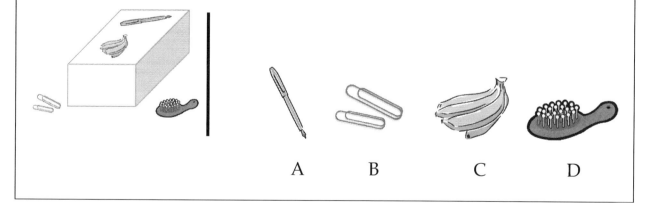

16. See the image below on the left side of the vertical line. Which object is 2nd from the left side of the 4 objects?

A   B   C   D

Section 4: Figural Reasoning

Section 4: Figural Reasoning

Instructions:

Read the question below and see the images.

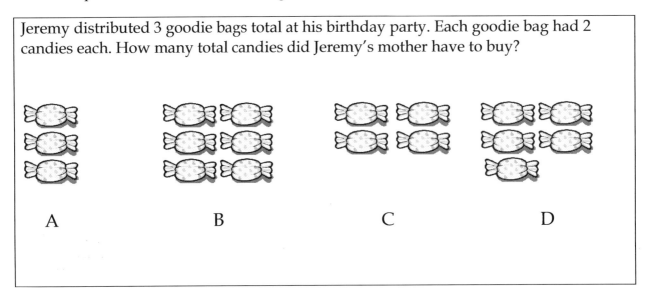

Jeremy distributed 3 goodie bags total at his birthday party. Each goodie bag had 2 candies each. How many total candies did Jeremy's mother have to buy?

A   B   C   D

The correct answer here is Option B because 6 candies would be required to put 2 candies each in 3 goodie bags.

All the questions in this section can be solved in the same manner.

1. See all the 4 images below. There are some arrow pointing in many directions .Which arrow points to the left side?

A   B   C   D

2. Terry went to the zoo with his mother and brother. When they approached the monkey cage, the zoo keeper said, they could feed the monkey bananas. The only condition was that they peeled the skin and then threw the bananas into the cage of the monkey. Which of the diagrams shows a half peeled banana?

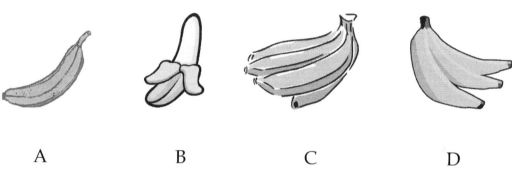

A   B   C   D

3. Adele was planning to go visit her grandmother and grandfather and take some flowers for both of them. She was planning to give them 2 flowers each. How many flowers should she take with her?

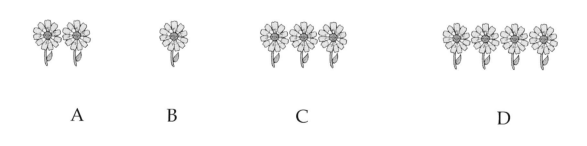

A   B   C   D

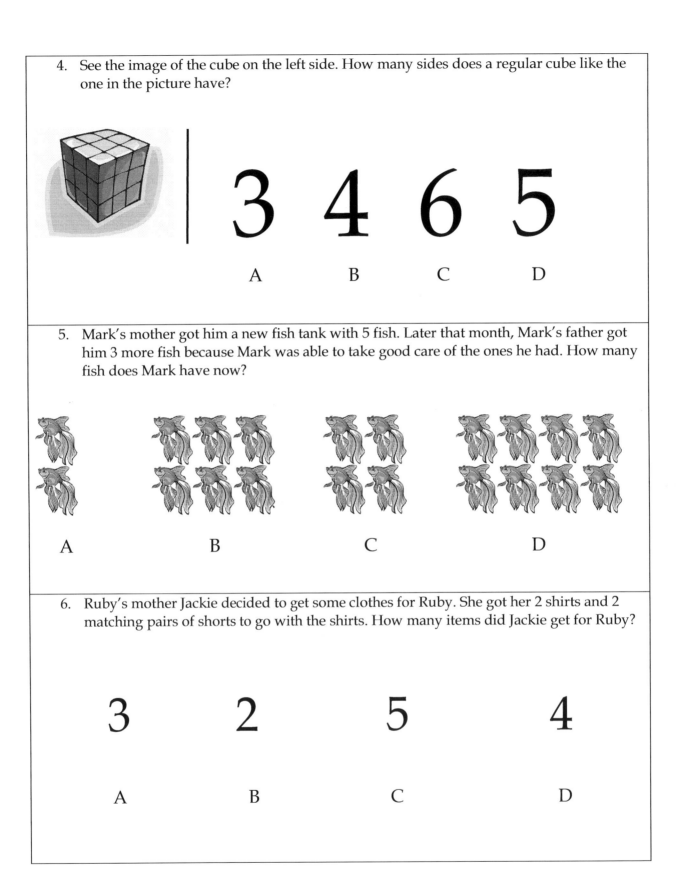

4. See the image of the cube on the left side. How many sides does a regular cube like the one in the picture have?

3   4   6   5

A   B   C   D

5. Mark's mother got him a new fish tank with 5 fish. Later that month, Mark's father got him 3 more fish because Mark was able to take good care of the ones he had. How many fish does Mark have now?

A   B   C   D

6. Ruby's mother Jackie decided to get some clothes for Ruby. She got her 2 shirts and 2 matching pairs of shorts to go with the shirts. How many items did Jackie get for Ruby?

3   2   5   4

A   B   C   D

7. Caroline loved to dance to pop songs on the radio. On any specific day, she dances to 2 songs on the radio, each of these songs lasted 3 minutes each. How many minutes did she dance in one day?

3	4	5	6
A	B	C	D

8. Mary, Jesse and Jack are three good friends. They went to the state fair with Mary's mother. After playing at the fair. They won 12 dum-dums total together in one of the games. How many dum-dums can each person get if they decided to split the award evenly among kids?

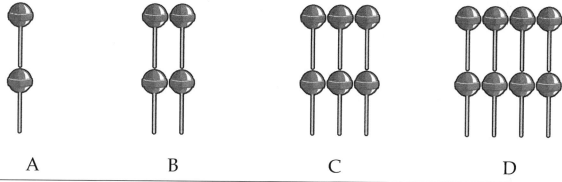

A	B	C	D

9. Bethany's mother got her 2 boxes of the colored pencils shown below. Each box has 4 pencils. How many total pencils does she have?

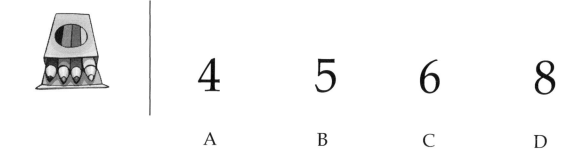

4	5	6	8
A	B	C	D

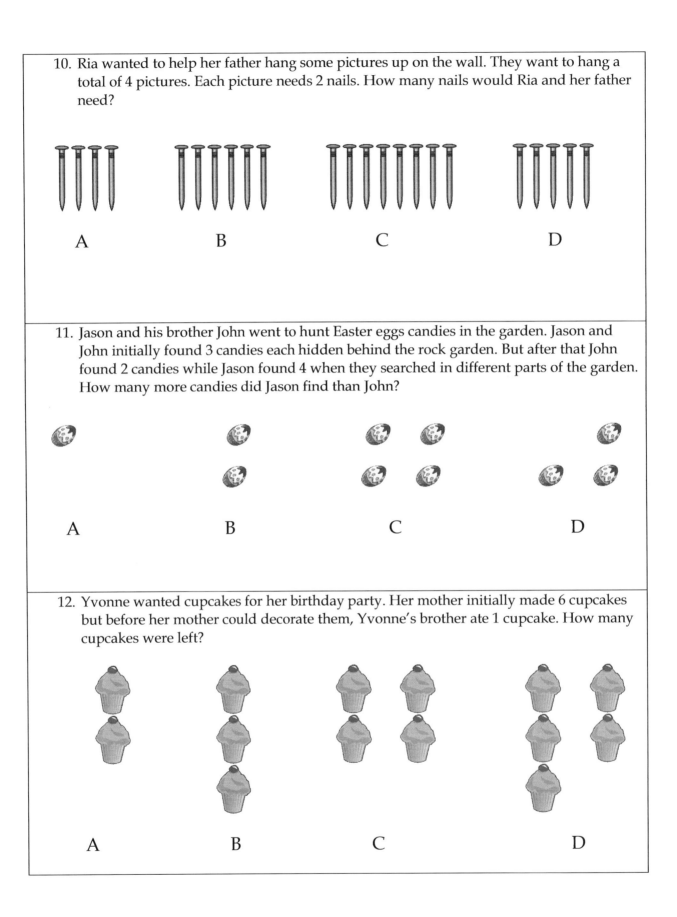

10. Ria wanted to help her father hang some pictures up on the wall. They want to hang a total of 4 pictures. Each picture needs 2 nails. How many nails would Ria and her father need?

A   B   C   D

11. Jason and his brother John went to hunt Easter eggs candies in the garden. Jason and John initially found 3 candies each hidden behind the rock garden. But after that John found 2 candies while Jason found 4 when they searched in different parts of the garden. How many more candies did Jason find than John?

A   B   C   D

12. Yvonne wanted cupcakes for her birthday party. Her mother initially made 6 cupcakes but before her mother could decorate them, Yvonne's brother ate 1 cupcake. How many cupcakes were left?

A   B   C   D

13. Which of the following objects is *not* round and cannot roll around on the ground?

A   B   C   D

14. Which of the 4 arrows would be appropriate in the blank square on the left?

A   B   C   D

15. Which of the 4 object would be appropriate in the blank square on the left?

A   B   C   D

16. Which of the 4 objects would be appropriate in the blank square on the left?

A   B   C   D

17. Which of the 4 objects would be appropriate in the blank square on the left?

A   B   C   D

18. Here is the picture of a family. There is a son, father, daughter and mother. Who is the tallest in the family?

A   B   C   D

19. See the 4 arrows below. Which arrow points to North and South Direction?

A   **B**   **C**   **D**

20. Which of the 4 objects would be appropriate in the blank square on the left?

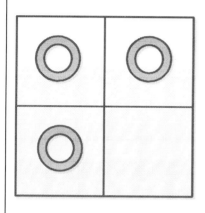   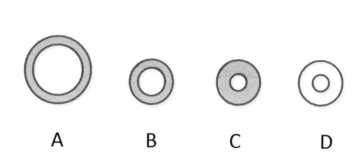

A   B   C   D

Blank Answer Sheets

Name: _____   Date: _____

Practice Test #1

Section 1

1 (A) (B) (C) (D)
2 (A) (B) (C) (D)
3 (A) (B) (C) (D)
4 (A) (B) (C) (D)
5 (A) (B) (C) (D)
6 (A) (B) (C) (D)
7 (A) (B) (C) (D)
8 (A) (B) (C) (D)
9 (A) (B) (C) (D)
10 (A) (B) (C) (D)
11 (A) (B) (C) (D)
12 (A) (B) (C) (D)

Section 2

1 (A) (B) (C) (D)
2 (A) (B) (C) (D)
3 (A) (B) (C) (D)
4 (A) (B) (C) (D)
5 (A) (B) (C) (D)
6 (A) (B) (C) (D)
7 (A) (B) (C) (D)
8 (A) (B) (C) (D)
9 (A) (B) (C) (D)
10 (A) (B) (C) (D)
11 (A) (B) (C) (D)
12 (A) (B) (C) (D)

Practice Test #1

Section 3

1. (A) (B) (C) (D)
2. (A) (B) (C) (D)
3. (A) (B) (C) (D)
4. (A) (B) (C) (D)
5. (A) (B) (C) (D)
6. (A) (B) (C) (D)
7. (A) (B) (C) (D)
8. (A) (B) (C) (D)
9. (A) (B) (C) (D)
10. (A) (B) (C) (D)
11. (A) (B) (C) (D)
12. (A) (B) (C) (D)
13. (A) (B) (C) (D)
14. (A) (B) (C) (D)
15. (A) (B) (C) (D)
16. (A) (B) (C) (D)

Section 4

1. (A) (B) (C) (D)
2. (A) (B) (C) (D)
3. (A) (B) (C) (D)
4. (A) (B) (C) (D)
5. (A) (B) (C) (D)
6. (A) (B) (C) (D)
7. (A) (B) (C) (D)
8. (A) (B) (C) (D)
9. (A) (B) (C) (D)
10. (A) (B) (C) (D)
11. (A) (B) (C) (D)
12. (A) (B) (C) (D)
13. (A) (B) (C) (D)
14. (A) (B) (C) (D)
15. (A) (B) (C) (D)
16. (A) (B) (C) (D)
17. (A) (B) (C) (D)
18. (A) (B) (C) (D)
19. (A) (B) (C) (D)
20. (A) (B) (C) (D)

Practice Test #2

	Section 1						Section 2			
1	A	B	C	D		1	A	B	C	D
2	A	B	C	D		2	A	B	C	D
3	A	B	C	D		3	A	B	C	D
4	A	B	C	D		4	A	B	C	D
5	A	B	C	D		5	A	B	C	D
6	A	B	C	D		6	A	B	C	D
7	A	B	C	D		7	A	B	C	D
8	A	B	C	D		8	A	B	C	D
9	A	B	C	D		9	A	B	C	D
10	A	B	C	D		10	A	B	C	D
11	A	B	C	D		11	A	B	C	D
12	A	B	C	D		12	A	B	C	D

Name: _____   Date: _____

Practice Test #2

Section 3

1 (A) (B) (C) (D)
2 (A) (B) (C) (D)
3 (A) (B) (C) (D)
4 (A) (B) (C) (D)
5 (A) (B) (C) (D)
6 (A) (B) (C) (D)
7 (A) (B) (C) (D)
8 (A) (B) (C) (D)
9 (A) (B) (C) (D)
10 (A) (B) (C) (D)
11 (A) (B) (C) (D)
12 (A) (B) (C) (D)
13 (A) (B) (C) (D)
14 (A) (B) (C) (D)
15 (A) (B) (C) (D)
16 (A) (B) (C) (D)

Section 4

1 (A) (B) (C) (D)
2 (A) (B) (C) (D)
3 (A) (B) (C) (D)
4 (A) (B) (C) (D)
5 (A) (B) (C) (D)
6 (A) (B) (C) (D)
7 (A) (B) (C) (D)
8 (A) (B) (C) (D)
9 (A) (B) (C) (D)
10 (A) (B) (C) (D)
11 (A) (B) (C) (D)
12 (A) (B) (C) (D)
13 (A) (B) (C) (D)
14 (A) (B) (C) (D)
15 (A) (B) (C) (D)
16 (A) (B) (C) (D)
17 (A) (B) (C) (D)
18 (A) (B) (C) (D)
19 (A) (B) (C) (D)
20 (A) (B) (C) (D)

Answer Key: Practice Test 1

Section 1	Section 2:	Section 3	Section 4
1. B	1. A	1. A	1. B
2. A	2. C	2. C	2. C
3. B	3. C	3. C	3. D
4. A	4. A	4. A	4. A
5. C	5. C	5. A	5. D
6. D	6. A	6. C	6. B
7. B	7. A	7. D	7. C
8. B	8. D	8. B	8. B
9. C	9. B	9. D	9. A
10. A	10. A	10. D	10. A
11. B	11. D	11. D	11. A
12. C	12. C	12. A	12. B
		13. A	13. C
		14. D	14. C
		15. C	15. D
		16. A	16. C
			17. B
			18. B
			19. B
			20. C

Answer Key: Practice Test 2

Section 1	Section 2	Section 3	Section 4
1. D	1. C	1. C	1. B
2. C	2. B	2. C	2. B
3. B	3. D	3. D	3. D
4. D	4. B	4. D	4. C
5. D	5. A	5. C	5. D
6. C	6. B	6. D	6. D
7. C	7. C	7. B	7. D
8. A	8. D	8. A	8. B
9. C	9. B	9. A	9. D
10. D	10. D	10. B	10. C
11. B	11. A	11. D	11. B
12. A	12. B	12. B	12. D
		13. B	13. D
		14. D	14. C
		15. C	15. B
		16. D	16. C
			17. A
			18. B
			19. B
			20. B